This book belongs to

....

My favourite colour is

....

First published 2006 by order of the Tate Trustees
by Tate Publishing, a division of Tate Enterprises Ltd,
Millbank, London SW1P 4RG
www.tate.org.uk/publishing

Reprinted 2008
©Tate 2006
Photography, design and illustration © Ella Doran, David Goodman and Zoe Miller 2006

British Library Cataloguing in Publication Data
A catalogue record for this book is available from the British Library

ISBN-10: 1-85437-680-2
ISBN-13: 978-185437-680-0

Distributed in the United States and Canada by Harry N.Abrams inc.,New York

Library of Congress Cataloging in Publication Data
Library of Congress number 2006926562

Ella Doran www.elladoran.co.uk
David Goodman and Zoe Miller www.silence.co.uk

Printed in China by Imago

colour

ella doran · david goodman · zoe miller

Look around you

the world is full of colour

red

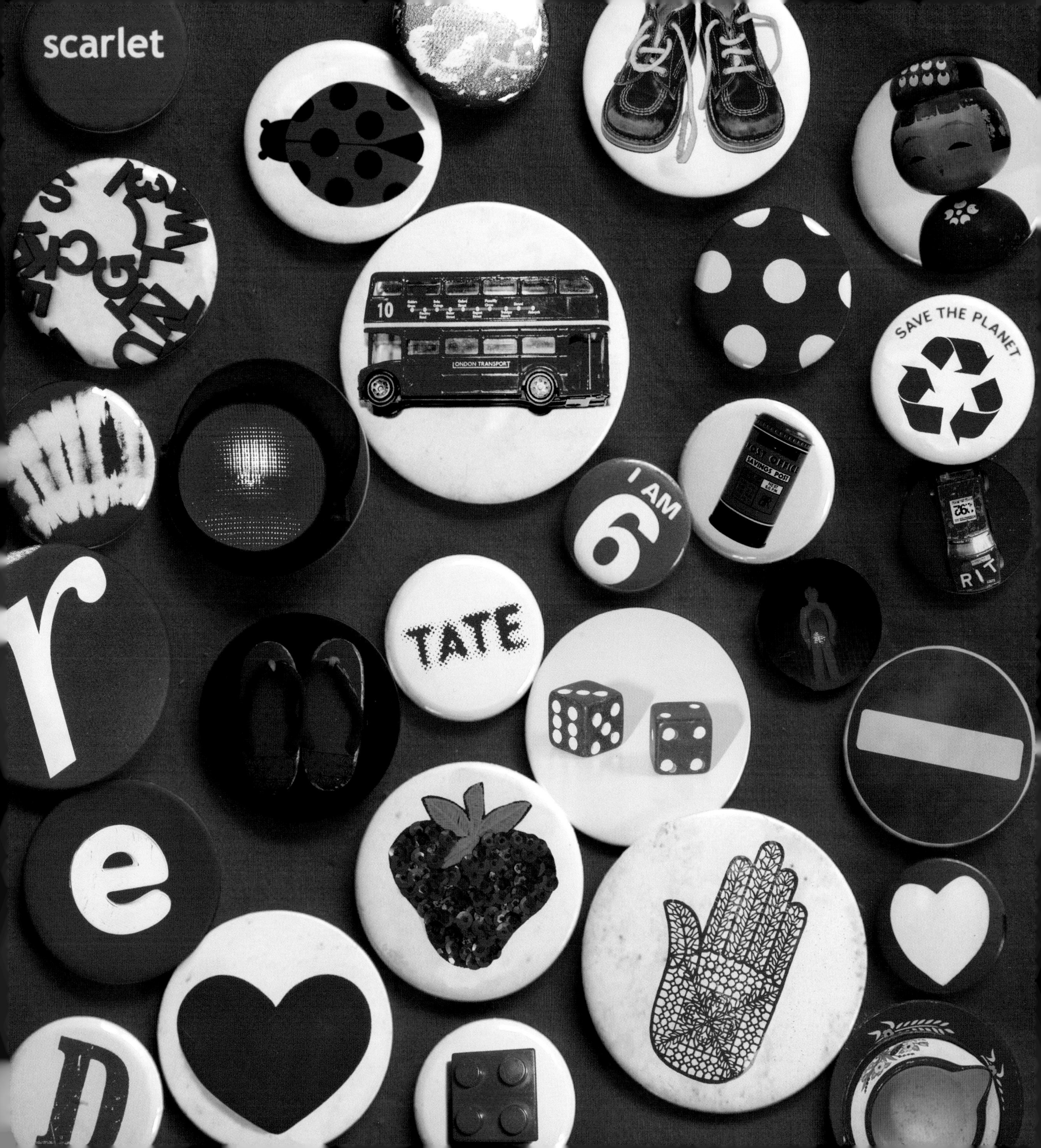
scarlet
LONDON TRANSPORT
SAVE THE PLANET
I AM 6
TATE
r
e
d

blue

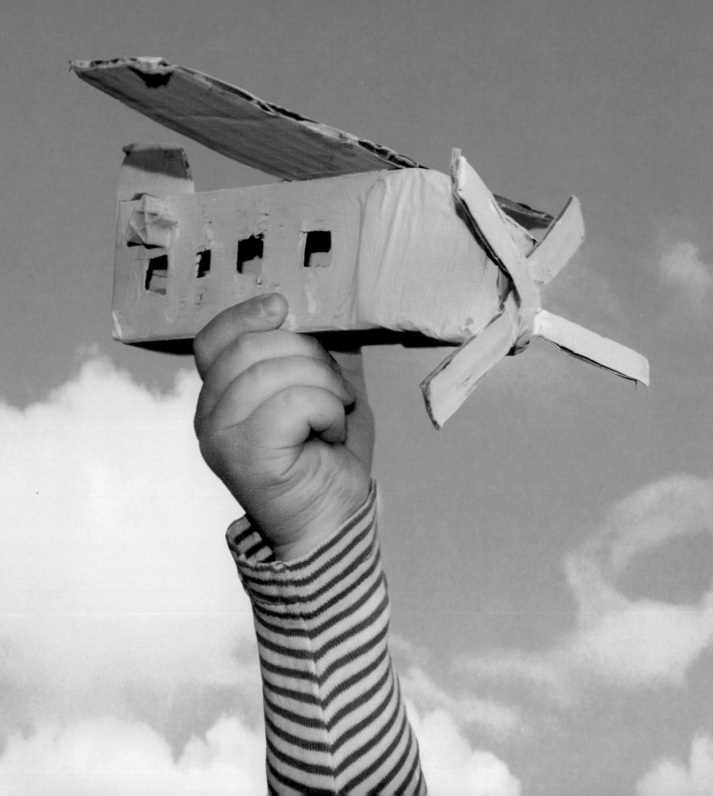

aquamarine

dark blue cyan

ultramarine pale blue

steel blue sky blue

indigo

cobalt azure

navy royal blue

midnight blue

powder blue

turquoise

blue

yellow

sunshine (repeated radially throughout the background)

yellow

THE SPIDER WHO TRIED TO EAT THE SUN

J Bird   **The yellow school bus**

H D LANG   THE CANARY WHO WOULD NOT SING

Alex Primrose   THE BIG YELLOW BOOK   lemon tree press

cheesy stories   by charlie chedder

primary

Red, yellow and blue are called primary, or pure colours. They cannot be made from any other colours.

You can mix two primary colours to make other colours. These are called secondary colours. If you mix all three primary colours you make brown.

secondary

● + ● = ●

● + ● = ●

● + ● = ●

● + ● + ● = ●

orange

purple

brown

Turn the wheel and see what colour you make when two colours are mixed together in equal measure.

Can you match each dab of paint to its name?

agenta sky blue pea green turquoise yellow lime
nnamon mustard poppy red navy blue plum pink green
ac fern green amethyst purple sienna violet asparagus
qua emerald forest green tangerine dark purple cream
ate crimson lavender pastel pink olive orange salmon
sberry pink midnight blue lemon yellow black ultra marine

mixing

pink·feminine·sweet·fun
red·hot·dangerous·angry·love
lucky·blushing·orange·warm
glowing·playful·bright·yellow
summery·sunny·cheerful
happy·green·growing·healthy
new·young·fresh·envy·blue
deep·cool·calm·sad·purple
powerful·royal·rich·brown
natural·down-to-earth·rusty
toasted·tanned·black·dark
shadowy·mysterious·night
grey·cloudy·dull·old·foggy
misty·moody·

Make a

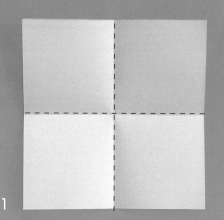

1

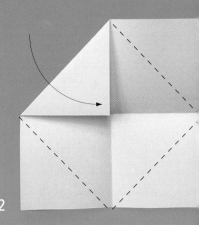

2

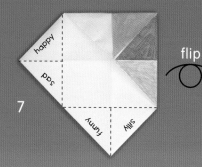

3

flip

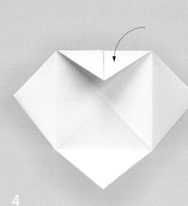

4

Fortune Teller

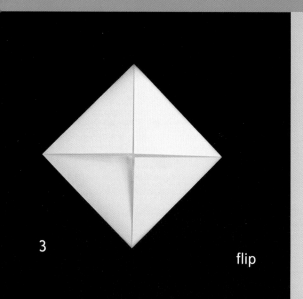

5

6

happy

sad

funny

silly

7

flip

8

How to make a Fortune Teller.
1 Fold a square sheet of paper as shown 21cm across.
2 Fold the 4 corners to the centre.
3 It will look like this. Then flip over.
4 Fold the 4 corners to the centre again.
5 Pick 8 different colouring pens.
6 Colour in the 8 triangles.
7 Write a feeling word that matches each
   colour under each flap as shown. Then flip over.
8 Colour each square differently.
9 Put your thumbs and fingers under the flaps.
   Move the outer corners to the middle to make a pyramid
   Pick a colour. Spell out the colour's name with the fortune
   teller by opening and shutting it in alternate directions.
   Choose another colour. Spell out that word too.
   Choose a third colour.
   Open the flap and see what it says underneath.

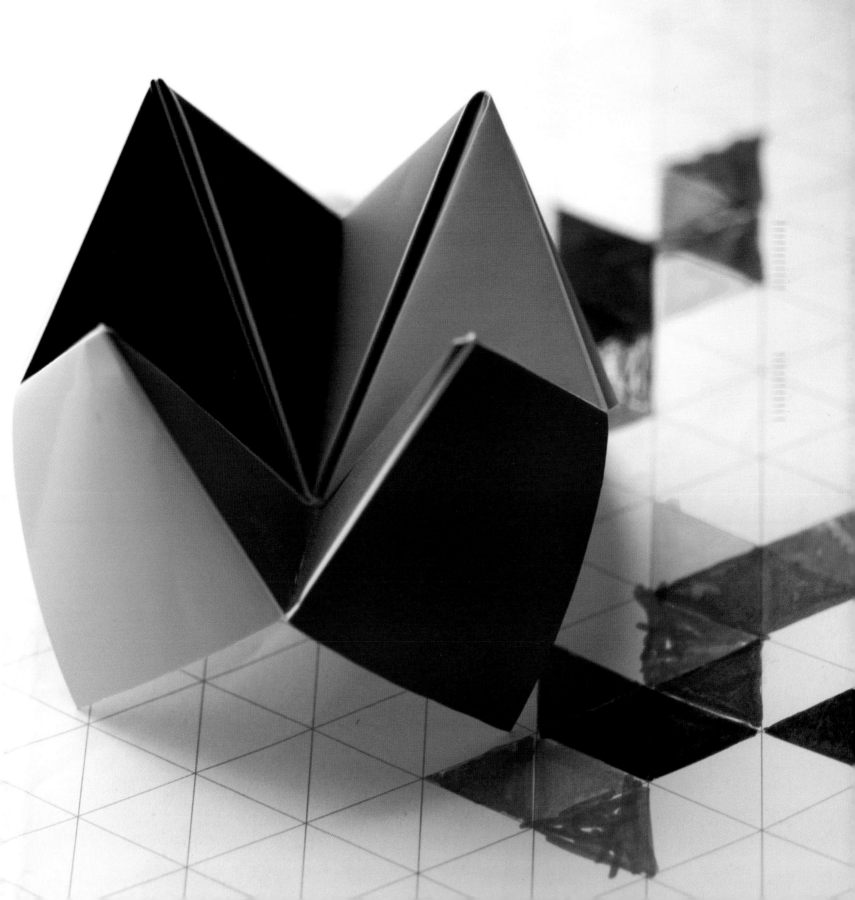

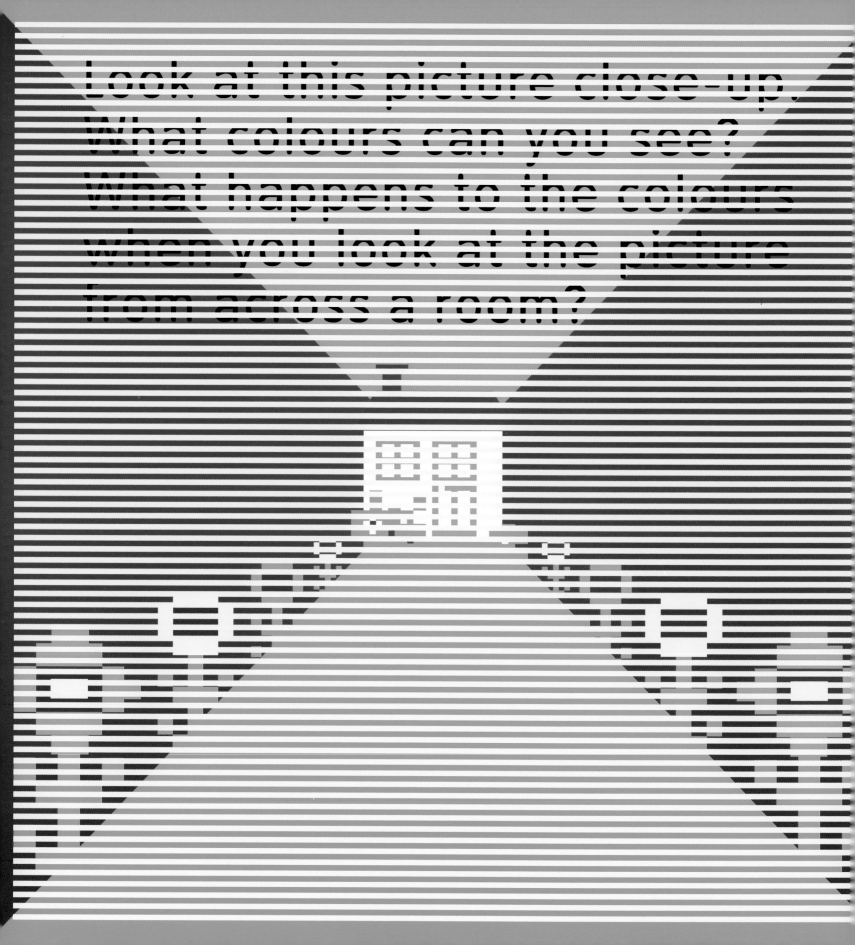

Look at this picture close-up. What colours can you see? What happens to the colours when you look at the picture from across a room?

white

BLACK

When there is no light, everything looks black.

the beam splits in

prism

Look at this page in the dark - what can you see?

A beam of white light is made up of colours.

If you shine light through a prism,

red, orange, yellow, green, blue, indigo and violet.

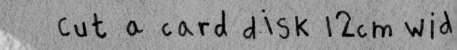
cut a card disk 12cm wid

Draw four lines through
the middle to make 8 wedges
all the same size. Colour the
wedges like this. Make a hole
on either side of the centre of the disk.
Thread string through. Make two loops.
Tie the ends together.

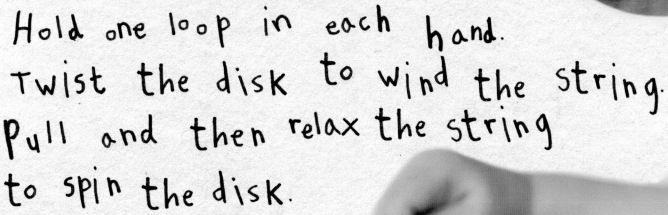

Hold one loop in each hand.
Twist the disk to wind the string.
Pull and then relax the string
to spin the disk.

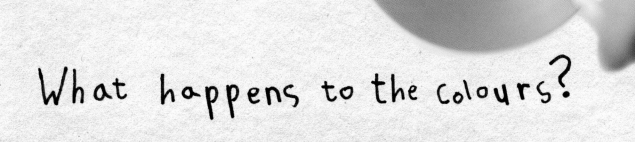

What happens to the colours?

TO
MAKE
A TINT
ADD WHITE

TO CREATE A SHADE

ADD BLACK

pink

Stare at this butterfly for 30 seconds. Then look at
the right-hand page. What colour are the spots now?

big or small

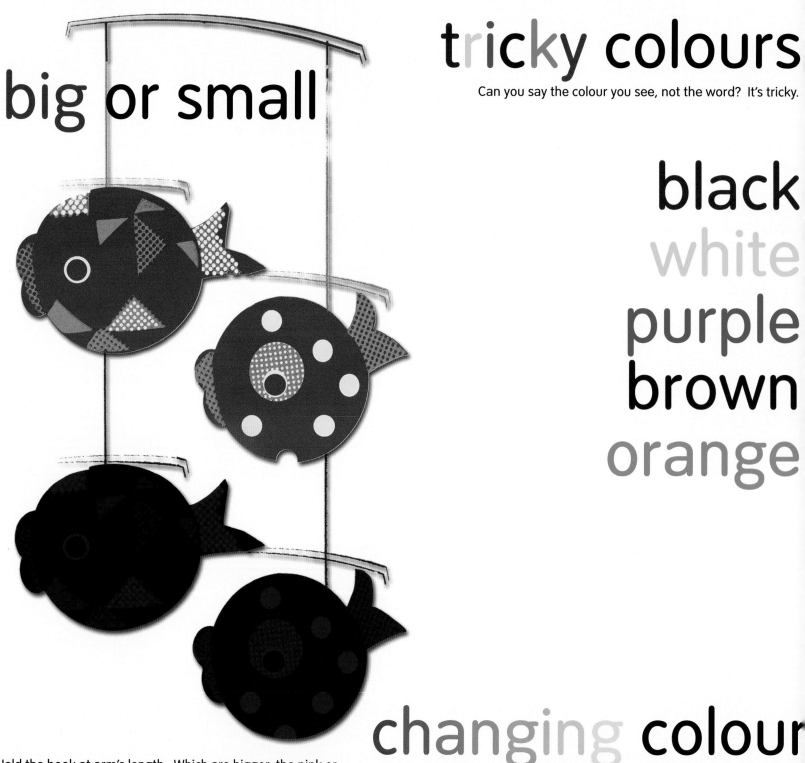

tricky colours

Can you say the colour you see, not the word? It's tricky.

black

white

purple

brown

orange

changing colour

Hold the book at arm's length. Which are bigger, the pink or the dark grey fish? In fact they are the same size. Dark colours make things look smaller and light colours make things look bigger.

Look at the pink line on the kite. Is it lighter at the top than at the bottom? Actually it's all the same colour, but the shading on the kite makes it appear to change.

red
blue
yellow
green
pink

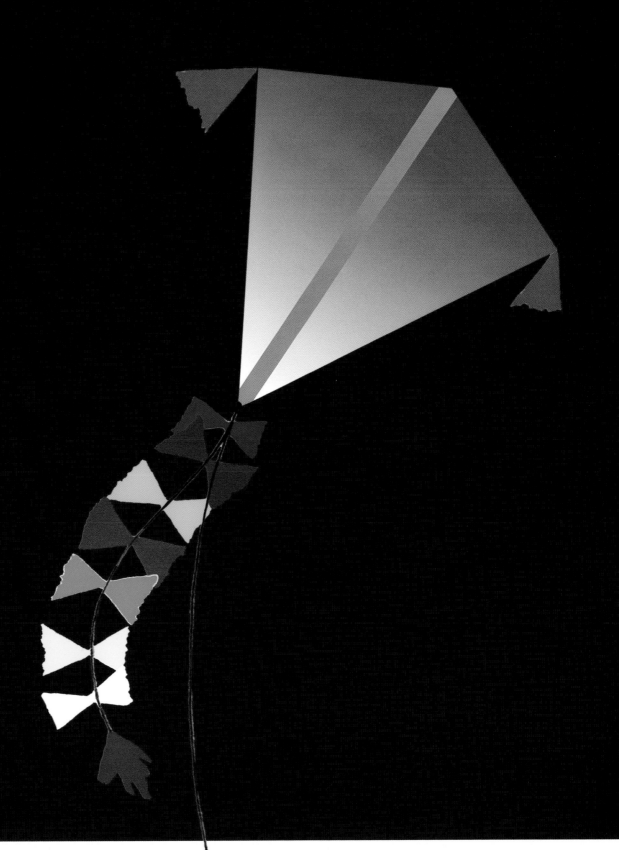

Some colours have the same name as a fruit or vegetable. Can you think of any?

Rainbows appear when the sun peeps through the clouds after a shower of rain. Raindrops in the air split the sunlight into seven colours.

Have you ever seen a rai

The colours always appear in exactly the same order: red, orange, yellow, green, blue, indigo and violet.

...ng through the sky?

A BIG THANK YOU

Zainab Abba, Olive Alvarez-Inwards, Kamran Amin, Blake Azim-Smith, Harry Baur-Harrison, Annie Botta, Carys Brewer, Nathan Brook, Fionn Claffey, Colourscape Music Festival Clapham Common: Lynne Dickens and Peter Jones, Elodie Curtis, Isaac Davey, Joan and Derek Doran, Rob and Jan Doran, Tashi Doran, Enyd Fracas, Louis Glass, Georgia Simpson, Calypso Garcia, All at Gayhurst Community School, Silka Gebhardt, Louis Glass, Robin Goldberg, Hannah Goodman, Joelle and Mara Green, Ike Greenwood, Vega Hertel, Millie and Kate Hill, Delilah Holliday, Sam, Saul and Simon Holliday, Ursula Holliday, Lauren Humes, Saira Iqbal, Olive Angel Jones, Amall Juma, Jeff Kazimir, Diana Kalungi, Moses Knights, Joni and Lola Leech, Mandy Maclean, Erin Mcdermott, Zoe Mellor, Tobias Miguel, Brian and Eve Miller, Saul Miller, Edgar, Lenny and Peter Mitchell, Benjamin and Yola Mutale, Lola Salem, Santilah Swan Piti, Emma Spinelli, Ruth Thomson, Heppni Wilkinson, Louis and Maisy Wynne-Roberts.